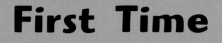

First Time

Going to the Doctor

Melinda Beth Radabaugh

Heinemann Library
Chicago, Illinois

Designed by Sue Emerson, Heinemann Library; Page layout by Que-Net Media™
Printed and bound in the United States by Lake Book Manufacturing, Inc.
Photo research by Janet Lankford-Moran

08 07 06 05 04
10 9 8 7 6 5 4 3 2 1

Library of Congress Cataloging-in-Publication Data
Radabaugh, Melinda Beth.
  Going to the doctor/Melinda Beth Radabaugh.
      v. cm. – (First time)
Includes index.
Contents: What is a doctor? – Why do you go to the doctor? – What kinds of doctors are there? – Where do you see the doctor? – What happens at the doctor's office? – Who helps the doctor? – What does the doctor do? – What tools does the doctor use? – What happens next?
  ISBN 1-4034-0229-9 (HC), 1-4034-0468-2 (Pbk.)
  1. Children–Preparation for medical care–Juvenile literature. [1. Medical care. 2. Physicians.] I. Title. II. Series.
  RJ50.5.R33 2003
  618.92'0075–dc21

                         2002155333

Acknowledgments
The author and publishers are grateful to the following for permission to reproduce copyright material:
pp. 4, 10, 12, 14, 15, 20, 21 Robert Lifson/Heinemann Library; p. 5 Mug Shots/Corbis; pp. 6, 9 Taxi/Getty Images; pp. 7, 8, 13, 16 Jose Luis Pelaez, Inc./Corbis; p. 11 Eric Fowke/PhotoEdit Inc.; p. 17 Ronnie Kaufman/Corbis; p. 18 Rob & Sas/Corbis; p. 19 Greer & Associates, Inc./SuperStock; p. 22 (row 1, L-R) PhotoDisc, Corbis; (row 2, L-R) Corbis, PhotoDisc; (row 3, L-R) PhotoDisc, Corbis; p. 23 (row 1, L-R) Eric Fowke/PhotoEdit Inc., Corbis, Corbis, Robert Lifson/Heinemann Library; (row 2, L-R) BrandX, Adam Smith, Corbis, Robert Lifson/Heinemann Library, (row 3, L-R) Robert Lifson/Heinemann Library, Corbis, PhotoDisc, Robert Lifson/Heinemann Library; (row 4) Jose Luis Pelaez, Inc./Corbis; p. 24 (L-R) PhotoDisc, Corbis, Corbis; back cover Robert Lifson/Heinemann Library

Cover photograph by Larry Williams/Corbis

Every effort has been made to contact copyright holders of any material reproduced in this book. Any omissions will be rectified in subsequent printings if notice is given to the publisher.

Special thanks to our advisory panel for their help in the preparation of this book:

Alice Bethke, Library Consultant
Palo Alto, CA

Eileen Day, Preschool Teacher
Chicago, IL

Kathleen Gilbert,
Second Grade Teacher
Round Rock, TX

Sandra Gilbert,
Library Media Specialist
Fiest Elementary School
Houston, TX

Jan Gobeille,
Kindergarten Teacher
Garfield Elementary
Oakland, CA

Angela Leeper,
Educational Consultant
Wake Forest, NC

Special thanks to Dr. Mark McHaney for his review of this book.

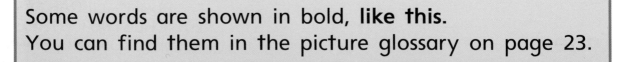

Some words are shown in bold, **like this.**
You can find them in the picture glossary on page 23.

Contents

What Is a Doctor?

Doctors know how bodies work.

They help keep your body healthy.

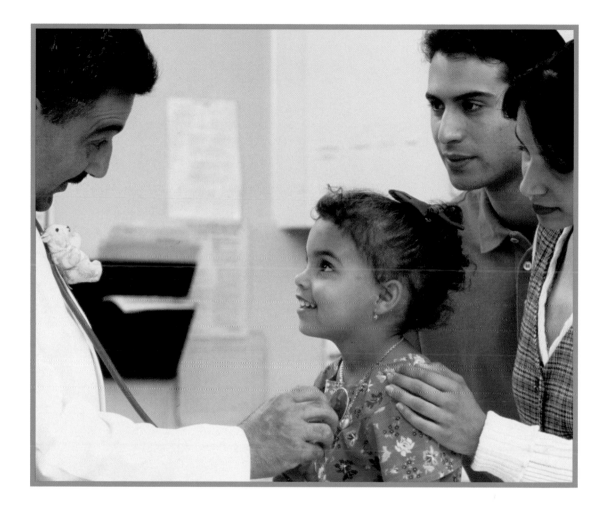

They check the inside of your body.

They also check the outside.

Why Do You Go to the Doctor?

You go if you are sick.

The doctor helps you get better.

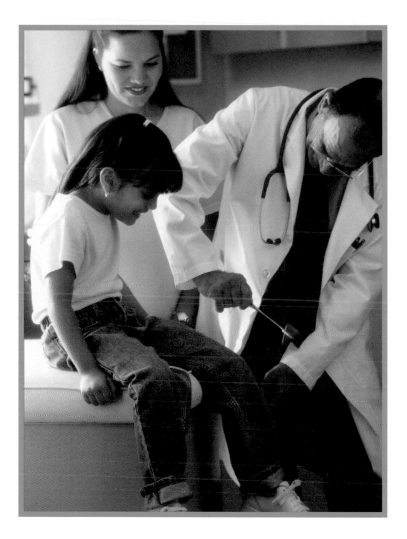

You also go for a checkup.

You need checkups to stay healthy.

What Kinds of Doctors Are There?

Pediatricians are doctors for children.

They take care of babies, too.

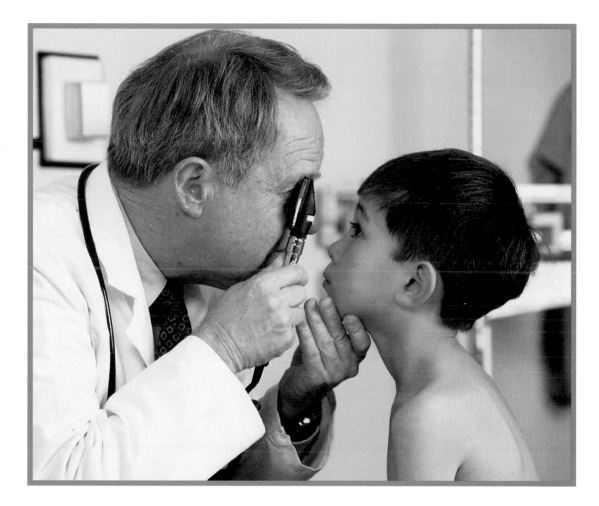

Optometrists help you see better.

They look in your eyes.

Where Do Doctors Work?

A doctor works in an **office**.

The office might be in a big building.

Some doctors work at **hospitals.**

Their offices are inside the hospital.

What Happens at the Doctor's Office?

receptionist

First, you see the **receptionists**.

They help you sign in.

Then, you wait in the waiting room.

Sometimes you can play with
toys or read a book there.

What Happens Next?

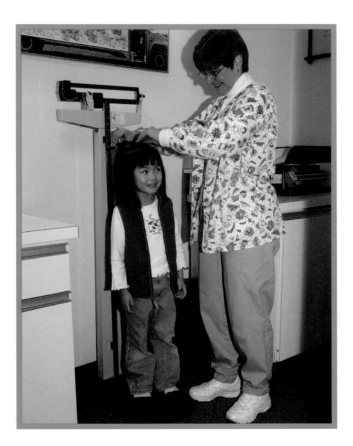

A **nurse** weighs you on a **scale.**

This nurse is checking to see how tall this girl is.

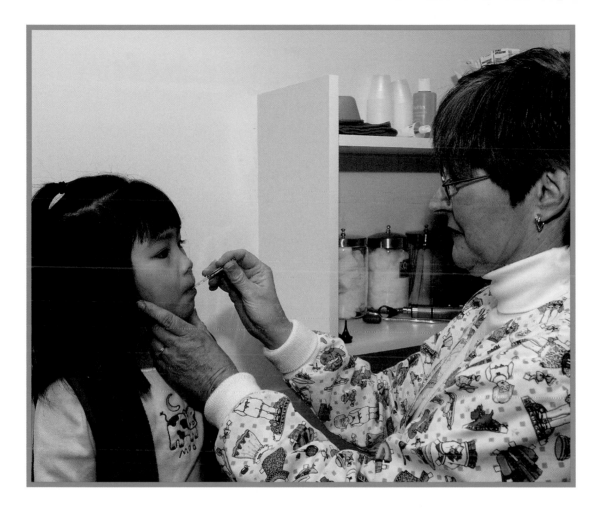

A nurse takes your temperature.

She uses a **thermometer**.

What Happens During a Checkup?

tongue depressor

Doctors hold your tongue down with a **tongue depressor**.

Then, they look inside your mouth.

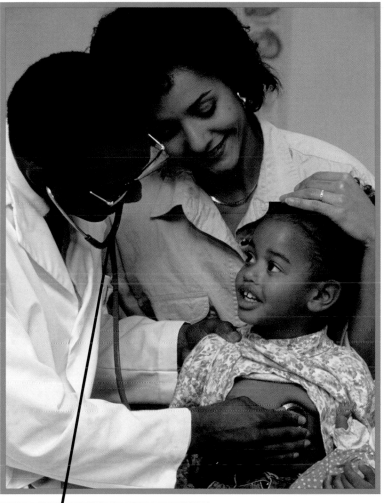

stethoscope

Doctors listen to your heart with a **stethoscope**.

What Other Tools Do Doctors Use?

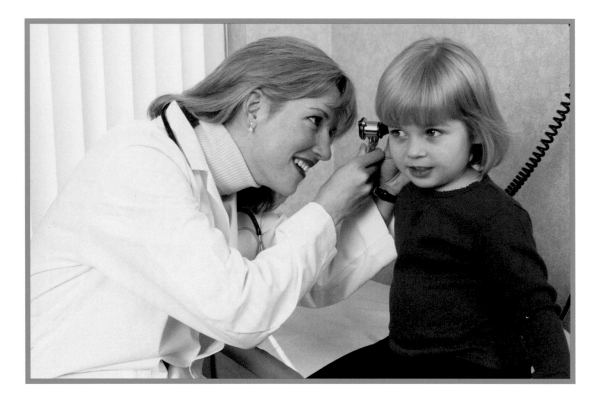

The doctor uses an **otoscope** to look in your ears.

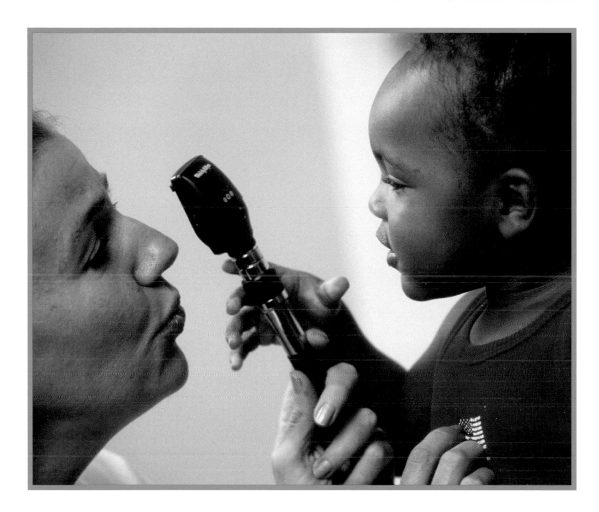

The doctor uses an **ophthalmoscope** to look in your eyes.

What Happens After the Checkup?

The doctor talks with your parent.

You might get some **medicine**.

You may get a special treat.

Then, you can leave to go home!

Quiz

What can you find at the doctor's **office?**

Look for the answer on page 24.

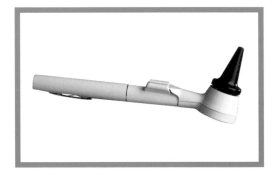

Picture Glossary

hospital
page 11

ophthalmoscope
(off-THAL-muh-skope)
page 19

pediatrician
(pee-dee-uh-TRISH-un)
page 8

stethoscope
page 17

medicine
page 20

optometrist
page 9

receptionist
(ree-SEP-shun-ist)
page 12

thermometer
page 15

nurse
pages 14, 15

otoscope
(OH-toh-skope)
page 18

scale
page 14

tongue depressor
page 16

office
pages 10, 11

23

Note to Parents and Teachers

Reading for information is an important part of a child's literacy development. Learning begins with a question about something. Help children think of themselves as investigators and researchers by encouraging their questions about the world around them. Each chapter in this book begins with a question. Read the question together. Look at the pictures. Talk about what you think the answer might be. Then read the text to find out if your predictions were correct. Think of other questions you could ask about the topic, and discuss where you might find the answers. Assist children in using the picture glossary and the index to practice new vocabulary and research skills.

Index

Answer to quiz on page 22

You can find the stethoscope, the otoscope, and the scale at the doctor's office.

24